THE BATTLE OF BRITAIN

Britain's Strong Victory
Against Nazi Germany

Written by Thierry Grosbois
In collaboration with Thomas Jacquemin
Translated by Rose Brichard

History | 50MINUTES.com

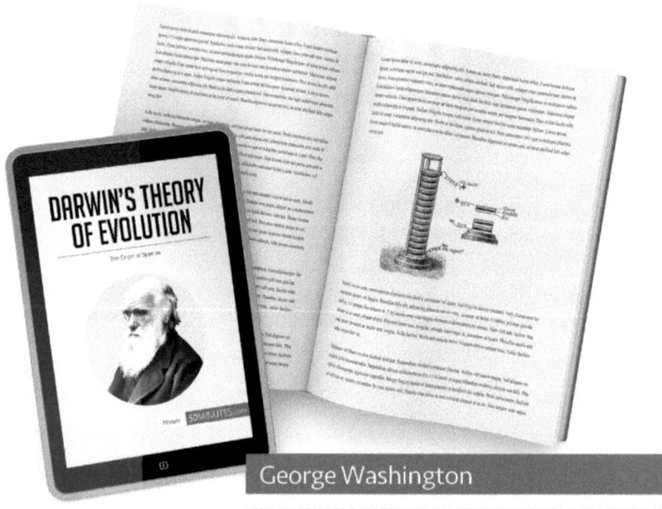

THE BATTLE OF BRITAIN

KEY INFORMATION

- **When:** Between 10 July and 31 October 1940
- **Where:** In Great Britain
- **Context:** World War II (1939-1945)
- **Belligerents:** Nazi Germany against Great Britain
- **Commanders and leaders:**
    - Winston Churchill, British Prime Minister (1874-1965)
    - Hugh Dowling, RAF Air Marshal (1882-1970)
    - Hermann Goering, German Marshal (1893-1946)
- **Outcome:** Victory for Britain
- **Victims:**
    - 1733 air crafts destroyed on the German side
    - 915 fighter planes destroyed, 450 fatalities among the RAF
    - 14 280 civilians killed and 20 325 injured in Britain

INTRODUCTION

Originally intended to foreshadow a Nazi invasion of Great Britain in Autumn 1940 which Adolf Hitler (1889-1945) postponed several times, the Battle of Britain was the most colossal air combat history had ever known. Hitler's aim was to destroy British Air Forces in the space of several weeks and laugh in the face of Marshal Goering's optimism. This would facilitate a German invasion of British soil; if the Nazis succeeded in crossing the channel, their victory in Western Europe would be complete. Once Britain had been conquered, Hitler planned to send troops back eastward to spearhead an attack on the USSR in spring 1941 to realise his vision as described in his 1923 autobiography *Mein Kampf*: Europe ruled by Germany where Communism was defeated and Eastern Europe was reduced to slavery. This was to be achieved through Blitzkrieg military strategy, where opponents' defences were quickly defeated through short intense attacks, Germany being incapable of sustaining a more prolonged war.

When the Battle of Britain began in 1940, Great Britain was the last European democracy to face up to the then-victorious Nazi Germany. This was, however, precluded by a major turning point on the British political scene: the pacifist Neville Chamberlain (1869-1940) was replaced by Winston Churchill on 10 May 1940, a man who supported a strategy of all-out war. This was the very same day that Germany launched an offensive, invading Luxembourg, Holland and Belgium. Churchill's authority would later be bolstered by a home victory in the Battle of Britain.

POLITICAL AND SOCIAL CONTEXT

THE PHONEY WAR

France and Britain declared war on Germany on 3 September 1939 after it had invaded Poland two previously without having openly declared war. A few days later, the British Dominions (Canada, Australia and New Zealand) followed suit and entered into the conflict. British and French colonies also would also take part in the war effort. In Europe, however, many smaller countries remained neutral and some of which would be attacked by Germany in April and May 1940. It was not until 10 June 1940 that Italy, led by Mussolini (Italian statesman, 1883-1945) declared its allegiance to Germany and entered the conflict.

The Polish Army was defeated by the Nazis in early October 1940, following the Soviet occupation of Eastern Poland on 17 September in accordance with the German-Soviet non-aggression pact. These Eastern regions, along with the three Baltic states would be occupied by and then annexed to the USSR.

Despite such worrying events in Poland, the major Western European powers did not react between autumn 1939 and winter 1940. The French and British governments were passive and immobile, paralysed by the wave of pacifism of the interwar years.

On 9 April 1940, Germany successfully invaded Denmark - a country which had declared neutrality - and attacked

Norway without declaring war. French and British troops quickly descended on Norway, but were forced to leave on 10 June after the Nazis launched attacks on Western Europe. The German campaign in Scandinavia gave Hitler access to high quality Swedish iron which would be used for the German war effort until the end of the war.

Reassured by an outright victory in Poland and Scandinavia, Hitler moved his armies westward, launching attacks on the Netherlands, Belgium, Luxembourg and France on the 10th of May 1940. The German Blitzkrieg strategy, based on a combination of military forces leading concentrated strikes on land and air forces, crushed France and its allies within just a few weeks.

On 16 June 1940, the French government, led by Paul Reynaud, was replaced by a new administration, with Battle of Verdun (February-December 1916) hero Marshal Pétain (1856-1951) at the helm. He signed a peace treaty with Germany on 22 June 1940 in Rethondes. However, the French General De Gaulle openly refuted the terms of the armistice and declared France to be a free country. This meant that Britain found itself alone in the face of Nazi Germany, despite most occupied countries' governments moving their headquarters to London.

BRITAIN STANDS ALONE AGAINST THE NAZIS

After France's defeat, the Third Reich found itself at the peak of its military and political power in Europe. Many neutral countries in Europe and Latin American opted to foster friendly relations with Nazi Germany. Meanwhile, the populations of occupied countries were still recovering from the psychological shock of the Blitzkrieg attacks and successive German victories. These populations tended to adopt pragmatic or wait-and-see attitudes towards the new occupations, trying to adapt to the new German order. In France, a smaller number of people nonetheless became involved in a resistance movement - known as the French Resistance - from 1940 onwards.

Soviet Leader Joseph Stalin (1878-1953), tried to avoid the Soviet Union being implicated in a European war and showed more and more signs and gestures of goodwill towards the German Third Reich. Across the Atlantic in the U.S.A., isolationist thinking maintained its prevalence, particularly among the Republican Party; public opinion showed significant signs of hesitancy towards any direct American military intervention in Europe. As such, President Franklin Roosevelt (1882-1945) had to delay any potential action, particularly given that the presidential elections were taking place in November 1940. The Americans were nonetheless alarmed by France's defeat and the threat Germany posed to Britain; surely Britain surrendering was not possible?

Intent on fighting against Germany with the help of the British Commonwealth, Churchill's government was thwarting Hitler's grand plan. In Hitler's ideal world, Britain would be quickly defeated and military attention could be focussed on the USSR so that Germany would not have to si-multaneously wage war on two different fronts. The Battle of Britain therefore represented a threat to the continued success Germany had been enjoying in its quest for territorial expansion since 1936.

Despite the numerous victories Hitler had achieved in Europe since the Munich Agreement of 1938, he was reluctant to thrust Germany into total war against Britain. Aware that such an action would pit his armies against the entirety of the British Commonwealth, he instead tried to come to a peaceful compromise, in the knowledge that the fall of the British Empire would only feed two growing world powers: America and Japan.

THE MUNICH AGREEMENT

When Hitler came to power in 1933, Germany began an intensive programme of rearmament with the aim of shifting the balance of power in Europe. In 1936, Germany began military reoccupation of the Rhineland territory, thus violating the Treaty of Versailles (28 June 1919). In the same year, the country entered into a war economy and embarked upon a project of expansion in Central Europe. This helped it re-establish itself as a world power, particularly in the face of Soviet and Anglo-Saxon hegemony.

France and Britain remained largely passive in the wake of such clear violations of the Treaty of Versailles, allowing Germany to take hold of Austria in March 1938. Hitler then demanded Sudetenland, a German-speaking region of Czechoslovakia, be annexed to Germany in what is known as the Sudetenland Crisis.

Hitler also had other plans. He hoped to end the German-Soviet Nonaggression Pact by launching a surprise attack on the USSR. If he emerged victorious from such an offensive, he would secure the crucial territory needed for the spread of the Aryan race. However, in order to achieve this goal he would first have to establish peace in the West to avoid fighting on two fronts. He told those close to him about his plan; they tried to dissuade him from such an idea.

On 19 July, Hitler announced to the *Reichstag* (German parliament) that he intended to negotiate a peace agreement with Britain. While Churchill did not directly respond to Hitler's request, British Foreign Secretary Lord Halifax (1881-1959) brushed aside Hitler's summons to negotiate peace in a message broadcast by the BBC. Therefore, on 31 July, Hitler decided to postpone the attack on the Soviet Union which was planned for spring 1941 in order to concentrate German efforts on crushing Britain and forcing the country into signing a peace agreement. This discourse of potential Anglo-German peace was not echoed in London, with the new Prime Minister Winston Churchill preferring a strategy of total war. Churchill managed to galvanise public opinion in Britain and further afield through his memorable speeches, and immediately sought U.S. support despite the country's declared neutrality.

COMMANDERS AND LEADERS

WINSTON CHURCHILL, BRITISH PRIME MINISTER

Born at Bleinham Palace, Oxfordshire in 1874, Winston Churchill was part of the British aristocracy. He was a direct descendent of John Churchill (English General, 1650-1722), the First Duke of Marlborough. His father Lord Randolph Churchill (1849-1895) was a radical Conservative MP who died relatively young.

Winston Churchill opted for a military career very early on, hoping to find glory in his chosen vocation. In 1899, he rose to fame as a War Correspondent in South Africa where he was imprisoned. After escaping, he launched his political career, earning the title of First Lord of the Admiralty (the political leader of the Royal Navy) in 1911. During his mandate, he strengthened the British Navy, making it the most powerful in the world as 1914 approached. He was forced to resign in 1915 due to the failed Gallipoli Campaign (25 April 1915 – 9 January 1916).

THE DARDANELLES CAMPAIGN

The Gallipoli or Dardanelles Campaign saw the French and British navies oppose the Ottoman Empire and turned out to be a total disaster. France and Britain sought to quickly seize hold of the Dardanelles - a narrow strait which is the only access to the Black Sea from the Mediterranean - in order to support the war efforts on the Eastern front. However, they underestimated the Turks, allied with Germany, and were unable to overcome ruthless Turkish resistance due in some way to a lack of planning on the Franco-British side. The Allies thus suffered a spectacular defeat which would have major repercussions on the British political stage.

Though Churchill was far from being the only one responsible for this failure, he nonetheless lost his title and had to settle for the role of Battalion Commander of the British Army until the end of the First World War.

In 1916, he commanded an infantry battalion on the Western front. He then re-entered politics and took on several ministerial titles from 1917 onwards. He was Chancellor of the Exchequer between 1924 and 1929, and became less and less visible on the political scene during the 1930s due to his politics being at odds with the pacifism which dominated public opinion in the interwar years. He loudly denounced Nazism and strongly supported British rearmament. When war broke out in September 1939 he was reappointed to his former position as political leader of the Navy by Neville Chamberlain. He was energetic in his leadership, known for his military expertise and his anti-Nazi convictions, and became Prime Minister on 10 May 1940. Despite his efforts, he was unable to persuade France to continue the war effort overseas after the occupation of Metropolitan France. Churchill was undeterred and decided to continue fighting, rejecting Hitler's peace offerings. Unable to stomach this situation, Hitler launched the campaign which would become the Battle of Britain in July 1940 to defeat the Third Reich's last real enemy in Europe.

During the war, Churchill held both the position of Prime Minister and Minister for Defence. He lost the 1945 elections, ceding power to the Labour Party's Clement Attlee (British statesman, 1883-1967). Churchill was re-elected Prime Minister on a weak Conservative majority in 1953, but ended his political career two years later due to health problems. He died in 1965 at the age of 90.

HUGH DOWDING, RAF MARSHAL

Born in Scotland in 1882, Hugh Dowding had a passion for aviation. As soon as he was old enough, he enrolled in Sandhurst Military Academy where he earned the title of Officer before serving in the artillery.

After having obtained his pilot license, he joined the Royal Flying Corps in 1913. The following year, he was involved in the first air combats of the Battle of France (10 May – 22 June 1940) which ended with France signing an armistice with Germany. After the war, he played a key role in forming the Royal Air Force (RAF) and helped develop British pursuit aviation. In 1929, he became Vice-Marshall of the RAF and was promoted to Air Marshall in 1933. He received a knighthood for his services.

When Churchill was intent on sending more RAF fighter squadrons to help France in May 1940, Dowding persuaded him to keep the RAF reserves in Britain to defend the home front, anticipating that Britain would be the German air force's next target. He adopted a shrewd defence strategy during the Battle of Britain in his leadership of the RAF, using his fighter planes sparingly through concern for his pilots' lives. Through this strategy, he protected his forces from being wiped out by the *Luftwaffe* (German air force) and made any German landing virtually impossible.

He retired in 1942 and was recognised as the Battle of Britain's military mastermind a year later when he became Lord Dowding. He was succeeded by Marshal Charles Portal (1893-1971), whose strategic long-range bombings helped launch a new era in military aviation.

Dowding died in 1970.

HERMANN GOERING, GERMAN AIR MARSHAL

Born in Rosenheim, Bavaria in 1893, Hermann Goering was lazy and undisciplined as a child. As such, his father sent him to the Karlsruhe Cadets Academy where he achieved excellent grades, graduating in 1911.

As an Officer for the Imperial Army, Goering was part of the infantry fighting in the 1914 combats before asking to be transferred to a fighter squadron. He gradually achieved more and more air combat victories and became one of the Imperial Air Force's best pilots. When Germany was defeated, he publicly opposed the Communists and Republicans seeking to rise to power. He was forced to leave Germany and live and work in Denmark and then Sweden. In

1922, he joined the Nazi party in Munich after an encounter with the man who would change his life: Adolf Hitler.

He took part in the failed putsch in Munich as a commander of assault platoons on the 8th of November 1923 and was injured. After the injury, he became addicted to the morphine given to him to help his recovery. He returned to Germany in 1927 when amnesty was declared and began working for the Nazi party to help raise funds for German industry. He was elected as a Nazi political representative for Bavaria in 1928 and was re-elected two years later.

In the 1932 elections, he was promoted to President of the Reichstag. He served as Interior Minister in Hitler's first government and in 1933 let his troops wreak vengeance on their opponents. He founded the first concentration camps and created the Gestapo, which would be taken over by Heinrich Himmler (German politician, 1900-1945) in 1934.

He was appointed as Air Force Minister in 1933 before taking on the position of Luftwaffe Commander-in-Chief two years later. It was in this capacity that he entered the Battle of Britain in 1940, promising Hitler that the British Air Force would be reduced to nothing in a few weeks' time. When he was unable to deliver these promises, he was excluded by Hitler and his popularity plummeted. This was also fuelled by the fact the Luftwaffe failed to control European airspace and protect against the Allies' attacks on German cities.

He was sentenced to death in 1945 during the Nuremberg trials for the part he played in Nazi crimes. He committed suicide in his prison cell in 1946 shortly before he was due to be executed.

ANALYSIS OF THE BATTLE

AN AIR BATTLE IN SEVERAL STAGES

On 2 July 1940, Hitler reluctantly entered into total war against the British, whom he considered as cousins of Aryan Germans. His initial objective was to forcibly establish peace with Great Britain to leave his forces free to attack the USSR. Before the battle began, Hitler's overall plan was to defeat Britain through submarine warfare and isolate the island from its sources of supply. However, Air Marshall Hermann Goering started a campaign to reduce British air defences to nothing through massive Luftwaffe attacks.

It was not until mid-July that Hitler gave instructions to his military forces to prepare around ten divisions to penetrate British coasts in autumn 1940. In order to put this plan, named Operation Sea Lion" (*seelöwe* in the German), into action, the Germans would have to control British airspace. The air combat, which became more and more intense throughout the summer of 1940, was only stage part of a larger plan to invade British soil.

Three branches of the air force based in Norway, Holland, Belgium and Northern France led the initial strikes against Britain, which altogether featured 3196 planes including several Italian squadrons. However, the German Air Force had two great weaknesses: the *Stukas* and the bomber planes. Stukas were the same dive-bombing aircrafts that had terrorised the streets of Poland and France in 1939 and 1940, but which proved to be vulnerable to British fighter jets.

As such, they were quickly put out of combat to serve as support to the troops who would lead the invasion. German bomber planes on the other hand were designed for tactical use. They were fast but badly-armed and fragile, only able to hold two tonnes of bombs. Therefore, they were incapable of carrying out strategic mass bombings to the scale that American and British long-range action aircrafts would reach in the second half of the war.

The German air campaign against Britain was composed of three successive stages which show the German High Command's hesitations regarding to the strategic objectives pursued:

- The first phase (10 July – 18 August) prioritised attacks on convoys of merchant ships in the English Channel and tried to cause disturbances at British ports in the South of England to lead British fighter jets into a trap which would see them wiped out, leaving the navy vulnerable to the ensuing destruction.
- The second phase (24 August – 27 September) arose from Hitler's decision to concentrate all combat on London. The Luftwaffe tried to open an air route towards London, wipe out the aircrafts protecting the city and destroy the airports. This would clear the road for a mass bombing which would demoralise the British population.
- Due to the Luftwaffe's failure to destroy the RAF and the decision to postpone an army-led invasion, the third phase consisted of blindly bombing London and other major cities.

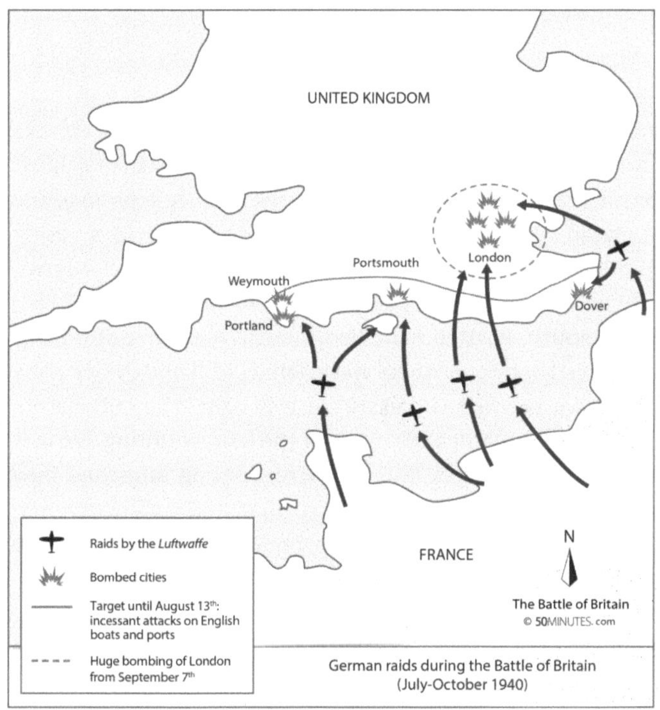

German raids during the Battle of Britain
(July-October 1940)

GOOD TO KNOW

Though fighting officially began on 10 July, Germany began its first assaults on the British Isles before this date. Already on 4 July, a huge raid was carried out on the Isle of Portland which sunk a counter-air naval defence ship in the space of a few minutes and led to 176 fatalities.

A CATASTROPHIC ATTACK ON BRITISH PORTS

While the Battle of Britain began on 10 July, the attacks reached became much more intense from the 8th of August onwards. In an attempt to stifle the British economy, the Luftwaffe increased its attacks on naval convoys, using hundreds of aircrafts at a time. On 11 and 12 August, intensive bombing was carried out on the ports at Dover, Portsmouth, Portland and Weymouth. A radar station was destroyed and four others were damaged. Though Germany may have seemed successful in this light, the Luftwaffe's losses were greater than those of the RAF, counting 296 lost aircrafts to Britain's 150. As such, Goering launched new and massive attacks aimed at crushing RAF defences in the South-East and North of Britain, hoping securing a clear and decisive victory.

Adlertag (Eagle Day), the name given to 13 August, was a turning point in the action. The German side led four successive strikes on South-Eastern defences, while squadrons departing from Norway targeted the North, which Goering wrongly assumed was not protected by fighter jets. These squadrons targeting the North suffered the most crushing losses, to the extent that they were almost entirely eliminated from the battle. Air Marshall Hugh Dowding had in fact previously taken the time to ensure that all areas of British territory were protected, North and South. The RAF arrived right on cue at the correct location each time Nazi strikes were attempted, informed by data gathered in radar stations. The British side therefore managed to wreak havoc in enemy aircraft formations, the Luftwaffe losing 190 aircrafts compared to the RAF's 114.

While this was happening, the RAF continued to bomb French and Belgian ports along the Channel where vessels and German troops preparing for invasion were waiting, despite its low supply of resources.

A MISTAKE WHICH CHANGED THE COURSE OF THE WAR

Goering changed his strategy following the first losses sustained by the Luftwaffe, deciding to concentrate military efforts on airports, the aeronautics industry and enemy aircrafts. To reduce losses, the number of bombers was reduced while fighter jets were increased. From then on there were five fighters for every one bomber.

During the night of 24 August, London was mistakenly bombed. This deeply shocked the population, and Churchill immediately ordered a replica attack on Berlin the following night.

GOOD TO KNOW

The first bombs struck London on the night between 24 and 25 August due to a mistaken release from German aircrafts. The German bombers were in fact aiming at Thames Haven petrol reserves in the industrial zone, but several bombs fell by accident onto the city's docks. Churchill refused to accept such an attack and

Between 24 August and 3 September, the Luftwaffe led a campaign of strikes on British aerodromes and aeronautics factories, losing 380 aircrafts to Britain's 286 in the process. British forces were gradually weakening; on 4 September, the RAF only had 704 fighter jets left and they were almost at breaking point regarding the difficult process of replacing personnel and equipment. At this crucial moment, Goering changed his plans yet again, ignoring his men's opinion and pursuing an offensive campaign of bombing on London.

London was hit by the most brutal attacks yet on 15 September, in what would come to be known as the Blitz. The city-centre, the palace, the financial centre, public institutions, hospitals and churches were all hit in this blind rampage. The city may have been wounded, but British morale was unshaken. In fact, the British commitment to continuing war became stronger still and Churchill became a symbol of his country, unwavering in the face of world conflict.

Astonishingly, the Blitz had a positive effect on the RAF; since the Germans had decided to focus their efforts on London they had ceased their systematic attacks on radar stations and airport facilities, thus allowing the RAF to rebuild itself. Furthermore, with the Luftwaffe sustaining more losses, balance between the opposing air forces was somewhat restored.

POSTPONED INVASION

The situation became increasingly precarious for Germany, with Operation Sea Lion compromised by British strikes on the ports from which their troops were ready to invade. After 15 September, the Luftwaffe began bombing during the night, having failed in its main objective of controlling British airspace in the hours of daylight. As such, the planned invasion of British coasts had to be postponed. While on 3 September the invasion was planned for the 21st, on the 17th a decision was taken to postpone further in the wake of the failed air combat.

Furthermore, the German navy was only able to send eleven divisions in the planned first wave of invasion, finding itself without the necessary transport facilities for its troops. The operations themselves also had to be rethought; it was decided that they should instead be spread out over three days and target just one stretch of English coastline. Given these conditions and the failure to exert control over British airspace, Operation Sea Lion seemed unfeasible to the German military. On 12 October, Hitler postponed the invasion to spring 1941, his mind already turned towards preparations for sizable military campaigns against the Soviet Union and in North Africa in 1941. During the wait, many ships which were supposed to invade Britain were returned to service industry, fisheries and maritime and river transport.

THE BRITISH ARMED FORCES FIND NEW STRENGTH

The British Army was able to make the most of the few precious weeks which RAF resistance had bought it to reinforce its territorial defences:

- The Home Guard, composed of men who had not been mobilised, was created. Its members' mission was to protect the territory through helping the army in its surveillance and safeguarding duties, allowing mobilised troops to perfect their operations.
- Women were also called upon to fulfil the roles left empty by soldiers, such as office work, operational services in aerodromes, health and education services etc.
- Therefore, as October began, British metropolitan forces had, other than the Home Guard and its coastal surveillance duties, thirteen divisions and three armoured divisions at their disposal.

After the catastrophic French campaign and the Dunkirk evacuation, the British Army was re-equipped and retrained, ready to confront the enemy.

THE BLITZ

Unable to exert control over British airspace during the day, night-time bombings by the Luftwaffe became an everyday occurrence in London in October and November. The damages sustained were significant, but the British stiff upper lip ensured that life went on.

Since the Luftwaffe had bases in France, it progressively opened out its range of action through bombing central Britain and naval convoys. From mid-November, the attacks became less frequent but remained bloody. On 14 and 15 November, a bombing raid on Coventry claimed 400 lives and destroyed the whole of the city-centre, including the cathedral. On 9 December, London endured 24 consecutive hours of bombing.

However, despite the civilian bloodshed during the Blitz, these terrorist raids, aimed at creating a climate of fear and despair, actually had the opposite effect; they instead helped construct and reinforce the British spirit of resistance in the face of Nazism.

Between 10 July and mid-November 1940 - the most intense period of the Blitz - the Luftwaffe lost 1818 aircrafts, with the RAF losing only half as many. The British also lost fewer pilots than the Germans; since the battle was fought entirely above ground, the Nazis were unable to take back any pilots taken as prisoners. Furthermore, the British were also supported by reinforcements from the Allies from summer 1940 on. French, Polish, Czech, Belgian, Canadian and New Zealand troops joined the ranks of the RAF and even made up autonomous squadrons, divided by nationality. On the German side, the excellent pilots who had begun the campaign were gradually being replaced by younger aviators, who were well trained but lacked sufficient military experience, leaving them more vulnerable.

While German attacks continued during the first months of 1941, they were much less frequent than during autumn

1940. The planned invasion of the Soviet Union somewhat explains the periods of calm which ensued between the attacks, which were becoming more and more sporadic. The German air force turned its sights towards the Eastern front, where Hitler's desired Blitzkrieg would become a war of attrition.

A BLAZING VICTORY

British victory in the Battle of Britain was achieved through a combination of fighter aircrafts, radar and anti-air defence. The concentration of British fighters during enemy attacks along with their high speed resulted in the failure of the German air offensive.

Factors contributing to the Luftwaffe's defeat include:

- the way the Luftwaffe's efforts were dispersed
- the changing strategic objectives throughout the decisive phases of the battle on Hitler and Goering's whims.
- the lack of mass effect which would have allowed a large number of aircrafts to concentrate on a specific objective
- the lack of heavy long-range bombers with greater capacities.

The Battle of Britain was also a technological success. The *Spitfire's* manoeuvrability, with brave and well-experienced pilots at the helm, has cemented this aircraft's place in history.

IMPACT

GREAT BRITAIN, VICTORIOUS

In early autumn 1849, as the Battle of Britain drew to a close, Nazi Germany was forced to postpone its plan to invade British territory due to the Luftwaffe's inability to control British airspace in daylight. This invasion would never take place, Hitler giving priority to his planned surprise attack on the Soviet Union in spring 1941. Furthermore, British military defences were significantly strengthened from summer 1940 on, shifting the power balance and making the prospect of a German invasion less likely still.

THE USA GRADUALLY BECOMES INVOLVED

The unexpected victory in the Battle of Britain helped Churchill persuade the USA to support the UK in its fight against Nazism. American armaments, outdated though they were, began secretly arriving in Britain in July 1940. In September, Roosevelt agreed to give the Royal Navy 50 destroyers despite the urgent need to protect American maritime convoys in the Atlantic. This was, however, a tactical decision; it was entirely in the USA's interest to maintain control in the North Atlantic and Roosevelt was therefore obliged to arm Britain to help in the war effort.

This donation of armaments paved the way for Congress's adoption of the Lend-Lease Act on 11 March 1941, which gave the President the right to donate necessary provisions to any country whose defence is considered vital for the

United States. The economic mechanisms of the Lend-Lease Act were to serve as a model for the Marshall Plan, which helped Western Europe recover after the war in 1947. This plan, proposed by Secretary of State General George Marshall (1880-1959) gave US financial support to European democratic countries, on the condition that economic reconstruction would be fostered within a framework of European unity.

The British and the Allied war effort emerged strengthened, and was no longer at the mercy of immediate financial constraints. The Battle of Britain also helped reinforce Roosevelt's position in America - he was re-elected for a third term in November 1940. During autumn 1940, US isolationist thinking started to lose ground and North-American public opinion gradually seemed to take into account that Britain's fight for independence and freedom directly implicated American independence and freedom.

NEW HOPE FOR OCCUPIED COUNTRIES

The Battle of Britain is also a major psychological turning point in the collective imagination of occupied countries between autumn 1940 and in 1941. While all hope appeared lost in summer 1940, the fact that a country had managed to resist Nazi Germany offered a ray of hope to those seeking freedom and democracy. The systematic economic exploitation the Nazis had put in place in their occupied zones - usually at civilian expense - also sparked indignation and turned public opinion against their regime. It was under these conditions that the first resistance movements emerged in occupied Europe during the autumn of 1940.

THE LUFTWAFFE'S WEAKNESSES

The Luftwaffe lost its supremacy in European aviation in 1940, as illustrated by British night-time air strikes on Berlin on 28 August which shocked both Hitler and the German population. The material losses sustained by the Luftwaffe in British airspace during 1940 would, in time, prove to be irreparable. In fact, between 1940 and 1941, the Third Reich's air forces lost several thousand aircrafts and as many highly qualified pilots. This jeopardised all prospects of a future victory. Nonetheless, after the British victory, Nazi Germany was duty-bound to take on some responsibility for occupying Mediterranean airspace, as the Italians were unable to do so alone.

When Nazi Germany attacked the USSR on 22 June 1941, the Luftwaffe found had great difficult covering this vast new front. Despite numerous Soviet aerodromes being destroyed during the first weeks of the conflict, Soviet aviation would survive the Luftwaffe's attacks, particularly supported by the Lend-Lease Act when it officially entered into war.

THE END OF NAZI VICTORIES IN EUROPE

The Battle of Britain and its outcome prevented Nazi Germany from ending its short Blitzkrieg in Western Europe with outright victory. Germany did not have the capacities to engage in more sustained warfare, and its attack on the

Soviet Union in June 1941 not only opened up a second front, but transformed the European conflict into a World War. This in turn reduced the chances of a definitive Nazi victory in Europe.

SUMMARY

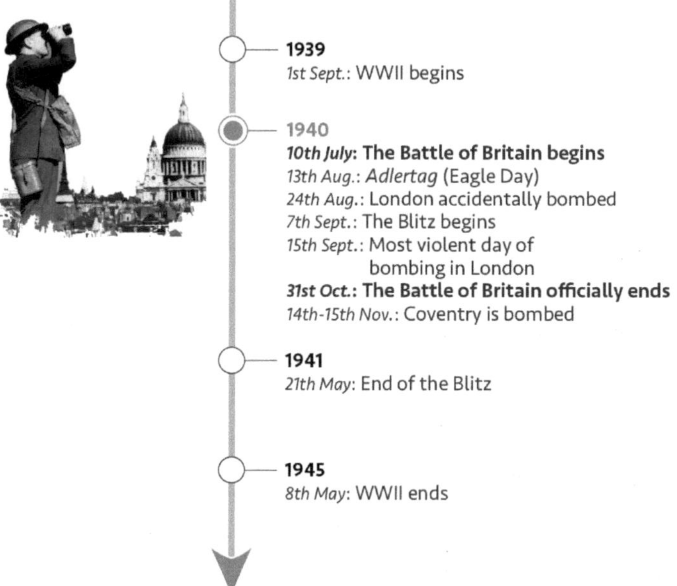

- Starting in 1940, Nazi Germany attacks numerous European countries. The French and British governments do not react despite having declared war on Germany. On 10 May, Hitler simultaneously invades the Netherlands, Belgium, Luxembourg and France; all of these countries fall within a period of several weeks. Britain finds itself alone in the face of Nazi Germany.
- Germany hopes to concentrate its war efforts solely on the USSR and therefore makes its intentions of brokering peace with the UK known. However, British Foreign

Secretary Lord Halifax refuses this proposition. Unable to accept this situation, Hitler decides to launch the Battle of Britain in July 1940 to force the Third Reich's last European enemy into submission.

- On 2 July 1940, Hitler reluctantly declares total war on Britain. A territorial invasion is planned for autumn 1940. To achieve this objective, the Germans must first control British airspace. Air combat with Britain begins.
- At first, the only targets are merchant ships and Southern ports. However, plans quickly change. Strategy changes would occur several times throughout the battle, particularly when the Luftwaffe failed entirely to destroy the RAF. Airports, the aeronautics industry and British aircraft are the next victims of German bombardment.
- During the night on 23 August, London is accidentally bombed. Deeply shocked, Churchill orders a reciprocal attack on Berlin the following night; for Hitler, the battle becomes personal. On 4 September, a furious Hitler decides to obliterate British cities.
- On 17 September, Hitler is forced to postpone Operation "Sea Lion" (territorial invasion of Britain) in the wake of the Luftwaffe's defeat in air combat.
- During the first months of 1941, German air strikes on Britain become less and less frequent, as Nazi efforts and resources are dedicated to the attack on the USSR. The Luftwaffe continues to sustain serious losses, whereas the RAF is strengthened by support from the Allies.
- On 21 May 1941, the final major German strike on Britain occurs. The outcome of the battle? German defeat and British victory.

We want to hear from you!
Leave a comment on your online library
and share your favourite books on social media!

FIND OUT MORE

BIBLIOGRAPHY

- Andurain, J. Bouhet, P. et al (2014) *50 idées reçues sur la Grande Guerre. Guerres & Histoire.* 18(April), pp. 32-69.
- Baudot, M. and Bernard, H. (1977) *Encyclopédie de la guerre 1939-1945.* Tournai: Casterman.
- Bédarida, F. (1985) *La bataille d'Angleterre.* Brussels: Complexe.
- Churchill, W. (1954) *Mémoires sur la Deuxième Guerre mondiale.* Brussels-Paris: Plon.
- Claasen, A. (2012) *Dogfight: The Battle of Britain.* Auckland: Exisle Publishing.
- Facon, P. (1992) *La bataille d'Angleterre. La bataille aérienne décisive de l'histoire.* Paris: Economica.
- Kersaudy, F. (2011) *Hitler.* Paris: Librairie académique Perrin. p. 135.
- Lespinois, J. (2011) *La bataille d'Angleterre. Juin-octobre 1940.* Paris: Tallandier.
- Liddell Hart, B. H. (1985) *Histoire de la Seconde Guerre mondiale.* Verviers: Marabout.
- Overy, R. J. (1980) *The Air War. 1939-1945.* London: Europa.
- Wright, R. (1969) *Dowding and the Battle of Britain.* London: Military Book Society.

ADDITIONAL SOURCES

- Barber, B. (2014) *Churchill and the Battle of Britain (Days of Decision).* Oxford: Raintree.

- Bergström, C. (2015) *The Battle of Britain: An Epic Battle Revisited.* Oxford: Casemate UK.
- Bishop, P. (2010) *Battle of Britain: A Day-to-Day Chronicle.* London: Quercus.
- Dixon, J. (2008) *Dowding and Churchill: The Dark Side of the Battle of Britain.* Barnsley: Pen & Sword Military.
- Overy, R. (2010) *The Battle of Britain: Myth and Reality.* London: Penguin Books Ltd.

FILMS

- *Battle of Britain.* (1969) [Film] Guy Hamilton. Dir. Great Britain: Spitfire Productions.

MUSEUMS

- The Imperial War Museum, Duxford Aerodrome (Great Britain).
- Royal Museum of the Armed Forces, Air Museum, Brussels (Belgium).
- Spitfire and Hurricane Memorial Museum, Manston, Kent (Great Britain).
- The Militärhistorisches Museum in Bundeswehr, Berlin (Germany).

IMPROVE YOUR GENERAL KNOWLEDGE

IN A BLINK OF AN EYE !

www.50minutes.com

www.50minutes.com

ISBN ebook: 9782806279170

ISBN paper: 9782806283085

Legal Deposit: D/2016/12603/316

Cover: © Primento

Digital conception by Primento, the digital partner of publishers.